First published in 2015 by
Clarity Media Ltd
www.clarity-media.co.uk

Puzzles created by Dan Moore
Design and layout by Amy Smith

About Clarity Media

Clarity Media are a leading provider of a huge range of puzzles for adults
and children. For more information on our services, please visit us at
www.pzle.co.uk. For information on purchasing puzzles for
publication, visit us at www.clarity-media.co.uk

Puzzle Magazines

If you enjoy the puzzles in this book, then you may be interested in our
puzzle magazines. We have a very large range of magazines that you can
download and print yourself in PDF format at our Puzzle Magazine site.
These include many single-puzzle titles including more sudoku
collections. For more information, take a look at
http://www.puzzle-magazine.com

Online Puzzles

If you prefer to play puzzles online, please take a look at the Puzzle Club
website, at www.thepuzzleclub.com

Puzzle Books

We have a wide range of puzzle books
available at **www.puzzle-book.co.uk**

Contents

Instructions

Combine Letters - Four themed words will be hidden in the grid. The clue will be given with each puzzle. Can you find them all?

Proverb anagram - the letters in each word of a proverb have been shuffled around, and the spacing also moved around. Can you rearrange the letters to solve the anagram?

Word splits - Combine the word parts to make 6 six-letter words.

Word wheels - Find as many words of three or more letters in the wheel as you can. Each word must use the central letter and a selection from the outer wheel - no letter may be used more times than it appears in the wheel. Can you find the nine-letter word hidden in the wheel?

Star letter -
2 star puzzles: Find a ten letter word that uses every letter around the outside once but uses the star letter twice.

3 star puzzles: Find an eleven letter word that uses every letter around the outside once but uses the star letter three times.

Themed anagrams - Solve the anagrams to find words related to the given topic.

Full anagrams - Find the number of anagrams stated for the given word.

Funny anagrams - Find the one-word anagram of the words given in each puzzle.

1 - Combine Letters

Find four sports by rearranging the letters below. Each letter is used once.

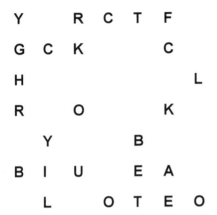

```
Y      R   C   T   F

G   C   K           C

H                       L

R       O           K

    Y           B

B   I   U       E   A

    L       O   T   E   O
```

2 - Proverb Anagram

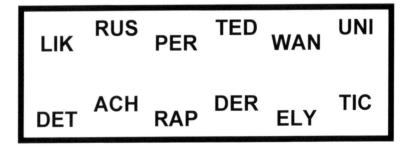

ARIDBNIHTE AHNDS IHTORW O WTNIH T EBHS U

3 - Word Split

Combine the word parts to make 6 six-letter words.

LIK	RUS	PER	TED	WAN	UNI
DET	ACH	RAP	DER	ELY	TIC

4 - Word Wheel

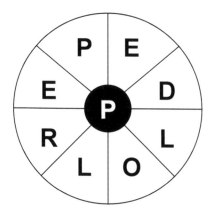

5 - Star Letter x2

6 - Themed Anagram

Can you crack these anagrams to find three words related to the topic of **African Countries?**

RAOCEMON

GIRAINE

ODIJTBIU

7 - Full Anagram

Can you find 4 anagrams of ESTER?

1-

2-

3-

4-

8 - Funny Anagram

LET BED MAT

9 - Themed Anagram

Can you crack these anagrams to find three words related to the topic of Animals?

LGAORTLAI

ETLEPHNA

DPNLHIO

10 - Star Letter x3

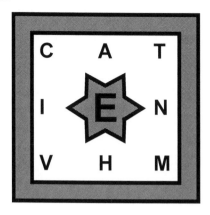

11 - Combine Letters

Find four countries by rearranging the letters below. Each letter is used once.

		A			G	L	
O		H	N				
E	I	P	W	U	R	D	
R	S	I			A		
A	D	T	A	L	A		
T		S			E	N	
		T		A	U	L	

12 - Proverb Anagram

A LPCA EOFR HNI ER G V YT E ADNEG VNR IHTYENIISTP E CAL

13 - Word Split

Combine the word parts to make 6 six-letter words.

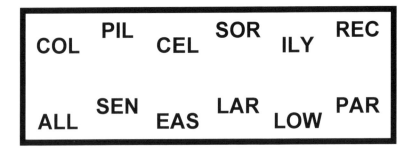

14 - Word Wheel

15 - Star Letter x2

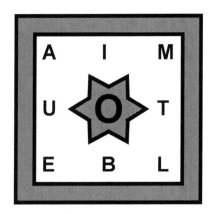

16 - Themed Anagram

Can you crack these anagrams to find three words related to the topic of **Baking?**

UHDOG

TAYPRS

IDNKGNAE

17 - Full Anagram

Can you find 3 anagrams of GNUS?

1-

2-

3-

18 - Funny Anagram

TIN GLEAM

19 - Themed Anagram

Can you crack these anagrams to find three words related to the topic of **Birds?**

TBRTIEN

WHPKAWRAORS

AMEIPG

20 - Star Letter x3

21 - Combine Letters

Find four colours by rearranging the letters below. Each letter is used once.

```
    W     N   R   E
I   H         E
L   R   P
W   O   B     T
P   Y   L     L
    U   E     O   W
```

22 - Proverb Anagram

ETHPNES II ETH MGIRHATN TE HSO DR W

23 - Word Split

Combine the word parts to make 6 six-letter words.

TAN	IFY	ECT	LER	RAT	ANT
CRI	ITE	FIN	AFF	SPY	GLE

24 - Word Wheel

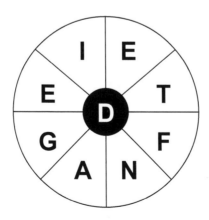

25 - Star Letter x2

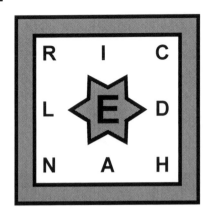

26 - Themed Anagram

Can you crack these anagrams to find three words related to the topic of **Butterflies?**

MRHACON

OBNISTMER

TTEIRSOOHLSLE

27 - Full Anagram

Can you find 3 anagrams of TIDE?

1-

2-

3-

28 - Funny Anagram

ANY OLD RIG

29 - Themed Anagram

Can you crack these anagrams to find three words related to the topic of **Christmas?**

SNCGTKIO

EENRSTP

ACRLO

30 - Star Letter x3

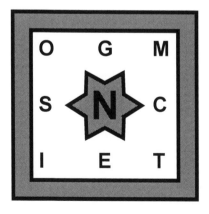

31 - Combine Letters

Find four tennis words by rearranging the letters below. Each letter is used once.

```
A   N   E      S

        E            A   C

    B   H      E         I

    S   L   D  V         A

B   Y

        L   R  N   K     R

C   I   E      A   L
```

32 - Proverb Anagram

ANOIRG L L NESTOS AR GETHO NS MO S

33 - Word Split

Combine the word parts to make 6 six-letter words.

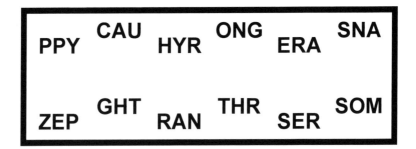

34 - Word Wheel

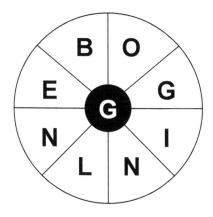

35 - Star Letter x2

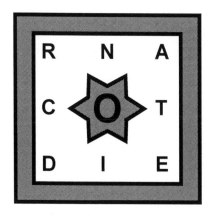

36 - Themed Anagram

Can you crack these anagrams to find three words related to the topic of **Clothes?**

EKTACJ

USOTRSER

PUVOLLER

37 - Full Anagram

Can you find 3 anagrams of SINGED?

1-

2-

3-

38 - Funny Anagram

DAIRY PIT

39 - Themed Anagram

Can you crack these anagrams to find three words related to the topic of **Colours?**

OIGNID

TURLAERMNAI

OGRENA

40 - Star Letter x3

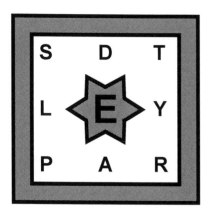

41 - Combine Letters

Find four US States by rearranging the letters below. Each letter is used once.

O   O   H

    T   R   Y   N   M   A

I   G   N   W   D

      I   O   E

G   O   E   M   N

S   O

N   A   I

42 - Proverb Anagram

HETRDSKT A EO UHRSI J SUT RBFEEOE THN A WD

43 - Word Split

Combine the word parts to make 6 six-letter words.

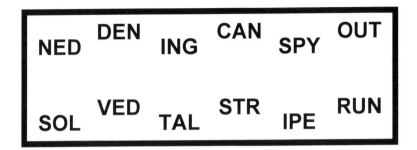

44 - Word Wheel

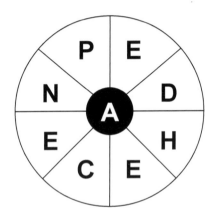

45 - Star Letter x2

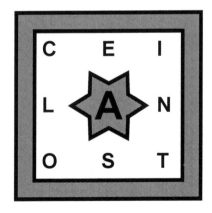

46 - Themed Anagram

Can you crack these anagrams to find three words related to the topic of **Counties?**

RURYSE

BHEIRKERS

EISHAPHMR

47 - Full Anagram

Can you find 3 anagrams of SECANT?

1-

2-

3-

48 - Funny Anagram

COD EATER

49 - Themed Anagram

Can you crack these anagrams to find three words related to the topic of **Countries?**

AATUIRSLA

LINBAAA

GRYNAME

50 - Star Letter x3

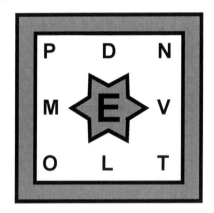

51 - Combine Letters

Find four items of stationery by rearranging the letters below. Each letter is used once.

E		S	R	A		
E	A	L			R	
C	H	I				
G	S		L		T	N
G	H	R		R		E
E		P		L	E	H
		T	I		I	P

52 - Proverb Anagram

L RAY EO T EDBDNA LYERA OTSE RIKEASMAMN AL, HA Y HETW TE AHY LNAD EISW

53 - Word Split

Combine the word parts to make 6 six-letter words.

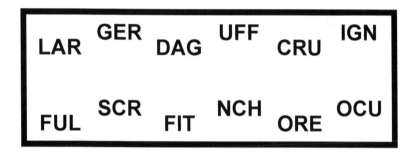

LAR GER DAG UFF CRU IGN

FUL SCR FIT NCH ORE OCU

54 - Word Wheel

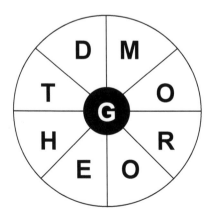

55 - Star Letter x2

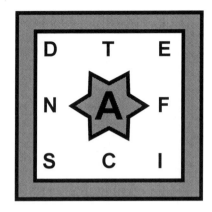

56 - Themed Anagram

Can you crack these anagrams to find three words related to the topic of **Cricket?**

KRORYE

YDUNRABO

PNISRNE

57 - Full Anagram

Can you find 3 anagrams of DECLAIM?

1-

2-

3-

58 - Funny Anagram

MANIC HOP

59 - Themed Anagram

Can you crack these anagrams to find three words related to the topic of **Elements?**

OANCBR

LUUNIMMAI

RGIOENNT

60 - Star Letter x3

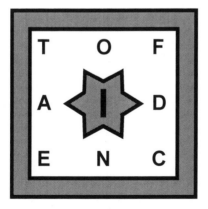

61 - Combine Letters

Find four trees by rearranging the letters below. Each letter is used once.

```
R  H  E  A      A
E  R  O
C  O  E     A
W  P         P
   B  N  R     M
Y  S  L  O     C
```

62 - Proverb Anagram

NIIMIA O TTSIEHTCNT RSI E S ER OFMF OR ALTET F Y

63 - Word Split

Combine the word parts to make 6 six-letter words.

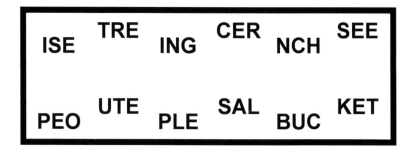

```
      TRE          CER          SEE
ISE          ING          NCH
      UTE          SAL          KET
PEO          PLE          BUC
```

24

64 - Word Wheel

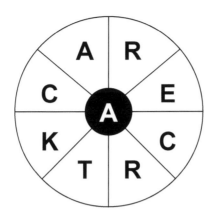

65 - Star Letter x2

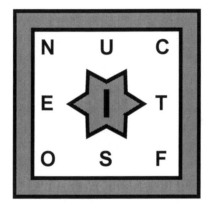

66 - Themed Anagram

Can you crack these anagrams to find three words related to the topic of **Emotions?**

ASSDSNE

XNETIYA

CESSAYT

67 - Full Anagram

Can you find 3 anagrams of FORTES?

1-

2-

3-

68 - Funny Anagram

OIL FAT CON

69 - Themed anagram

Can you crack these anagrams to find three words related to the topic of **Family Members?**

RTROEHB

NEAIRTOL

ERTAPRDAGNN

70 - Star Letter x3

71 - Combine Letters

Find four fruits by rearranging the letters below. Each letter is used once.

A	I	P	N	E
U	P		B	O
I		A	R	T	E
L		G	N	P
N		R	R	G	A
A	E		F	E	P
A	A		N	

72 - Proverb Anagram

AILETLT WEKLG NED OSIAOSRU GEADNGN IHT

73 - Word Split

Combine the word parts to make 6 six-letter words.

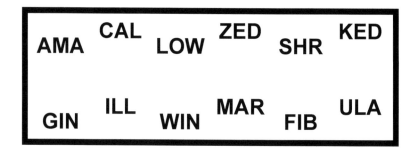

74 - Word Wheel

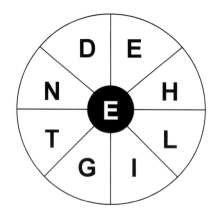

75 - Star Letter x2

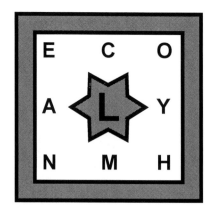

76 - Themed Anagram

Can you crack these anagrams to find three words related to the topic of **Flower?**

TECASLMI

MCNYCLEA

ODLFIAFD

77 - Full Anagram

Can you find 4 anagrams of MITRES?

1-

2-

3-

4-

78 - Funny Anagram

NO RETAIL

79 - Themed Anagram

Can you crack these anagrams to find three words related to the topic of **Football?**

EERFERE

EPEGEARLKO

FDFESOI

80 - Star Letter x3

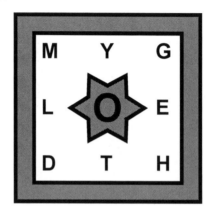

81 - Combine Letters

Find four mythical creatures by rearranging the letters below. Each letter is used once.

```
    O  G           Y

R          A

S  T     K  A  C  P

S  P  E  L     U

         S     C

K  U  E

E  N     N  C  A  R
```

82 - Proverb Anagram

ORME ODER HNOUN IETH BR CEHATNAHNIHET A S R N OEC EVB

83 - Word Split

Combine the word parts to make 6 six-letter words.

DED KEY JOC EVA TLY NUZ

EED EXC LAS ZLE RED HAT

84 - Word Wheel

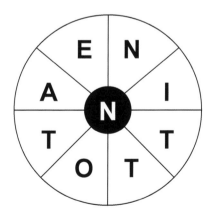

85 - Star Letter x2

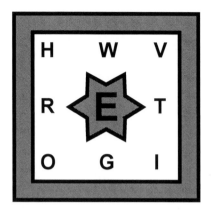

86 - Themed Anagram

Can you crack these anagrams to find three words related to the topic of **Fruit?**

OCDAAVO

NAANAB

TARIGUPFER

87 - Full Anagram

Can you find 4 anagrams of DERANGE?

1-

2-

3-

4-

88 - Funny Anagram

MOP CAN LIE

89 - Themed Anagram

Can you crack these anagrams to find three words related to the topic of **Gardening?**

NEWOAMRLW

ISEDNGLE

TOOSMCP

90 - Star Letter x3

91 - Combine Letters

Find four vegetables by rearranging the letters below. Each letter is used once.

```
U   R   T   C   T
E   O       T
T   E       L   E   T   R
O   L       P           R
G   C       A
    O   C   A       O   O
A   I   R       U   W   F
```

92 - Proverb Anagram

VN ERE OLKOAT G FI SOHR ENIHTEUT H O M

93 - Word Splits

Combine the word parts to make 6 six-letter words.

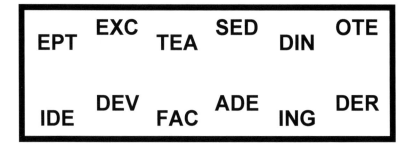

94 - Word Wheel

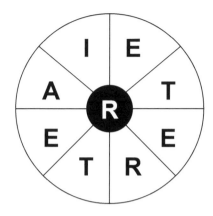

95 - Star Letter x2

96 - Themed Anagram

Can you crack these anagrams to find three words related to the topic of **Halloween?**

EUTSMOC

EPRECY

RESDPI

97 - Full Anagram

Can you find 4 anagrams of ALTERING?

1-

2-

3-

4-

98 - Funny Anagram

LAY ONE EGG

99 - Themed Anagram

Can you crack these anagrams to find three words related to the topic of Jewels?

QAERNAIAMU

OINMDDA

HAYEDOLCCN

100 - Star Letter x3

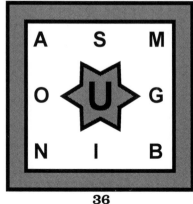

Solutions

1. Football, Cricket, Hockey, Rugby

2. A bird in the hand is worth two in the bush

3. Detach, Likely, Rapper, Rustic, United, Wander

4. Propelled

5. Absolutely

6. Cameroon, Nigeria, Djibouti

7. Reset, steer, terse, trees

8. EMBATTLED

9. Alligator, Elephant, Dolphin

10. Achievement

11. Portugal, Sweden, Australia, Thailand

12. A place for everything and everything in its place

13. Collar, Easily, Parcel, Pillow, Recall, Sensor

14. Amazingly

15. Automobile

16. Dough, Pastry, Kneading

17. Sung, snug, guns

18. LIGAMENT

19. Bitern, Sparrowhawk, Magpie

20. Citizenship

21. White, Yellow, Brown, Purple

22. The pen is mightier than the sword

23. Affect, Antler, Crispy, Finite, Ratify, Tangle

24. Defeating

25. Chandelier

26. Monarch, Brimstone, Tortoiseshell

27. Diet, edit, tide

28. ADORINGLY

29. Stocking, Present, Carol

30. Consignment

31. Backhand, Rally, Service, Baseline

32. A rolling stone gathers no moss

33. Caught, Eraser, Ransom, Snappy, Throng, Zephyr

34. Belonging

35. Decoration

36. Jacket, Trousers, Pullover

37. Deigns, Design, Signed

38. RAPIDITY

39. Indigo, Ultramarine, Orange

40. Desperately

41. Idaho, Minnesota, Oregon, Wyoming

42. The darkest hour is just before the dawn

43. Canned, Dental, Outrun, Solved, Spying, Stripe

44. Cheapened

45. Escalation

46. Surrey, Berkshire, Hampshire

47. Ascent, Enacts, Stance

48. DECORATE

49. Australia, Albania, Germany

50. Development

51. Pencil, Eraser, Stapler, Highlighter

52. Early to bed and early to rise makes a man healthy, wealthy and wise

53. Crunch, Dagger, Fitful, Ignore, Ocular, Scruff

54. Godmother

55. Fascinated

56. Yorker, Boundary, Spinner

57. Claimed, Decimal, Medical

58. CHAMPION

59. Carbon, Aluminium, Nitrogen

60. Edification

61. Sycamore, Rowan, Poplar, Beech

62. Imitation is the sincerest form of flattery

63. Bucket, Cerise, People, Salute, Seeing, Trench

64. Racetrack

65. Infectious

66. Sadness, Anxiety, Ectasy

67. Forest, Foster, Softer

68. OLFACTION

69. Brother, Relation, Grandparent

70. Ghastliness

71. Pineapple, Orange, Banana, Grapefruit

72. A little knowledge is a dangerous thing

73. Amazed, Callow, Fibula, Margin, Shrill, Winked

74. Lightened

75. Melancholy

76. Clematis, Cyclamen, Daffodil

77. Merits, Mister, Remits, Timers

78. RELATION

79. Referee, Goalkeeper, Offside

80. Methodology

81. Centaur, Pegasus, Cyclops, Kraken

82. More honoured in the breach than in the observance

83. Evaded, Exceed, Hatred, Jockey, Lastly, Nuzzle

84. Attention

85. Overweight

86. Avacado, Banana, Grapefruit

87. Angered, Enraged, Grandee, Grenade

88. POLICEMAN

89. Lawnmower, Seedling, Compost

90. Paradoxical

91. Cauliflower, Potato, Carrot, Courgette

92. Never look a gift horse in the mouth

93. Deride, Devote, Dining, Except, Facade, Teased

94. Reiterate

95. Pugnacious

96. Costume, Creepy, Spider

97. Alerting, Integral, Relating, Triangle

98. GENEALOGY

99. Aquamarine, Diamond, Chalcedony

100.   Unambiguous